Piano Camp

**Five Sessions of Musical Activities for the
Beginning Piano Student**

D1551110

PIANO CAMP PRIMER LEVEL is divided into FIVE SESSIONS, one session for each day of the week. Included in each session are activities relating to PRE-READING NOTES, RHYTHM, MUSIC SYMBOLS, LISTENING, SIGHT READING and KEYBOARD ACTIVITIES. Each session also has a page about music, music history or musical instruments.

Sessions may be divided for use in shorter time periods, making more than five sessions.

Sessions may also be extended by spending more time on the activities presented, playing more games and adding more activities related to music history.

Pages 42–48 contain games directly correlated to the concepts being taught in this book. At least one of these games should be used in each session. Suggestions for the appropriate time to use these games are found in the "Note to the Teacher" at the bottom of selected pages.

June C. Montgomery

ISBN 0-7390-0649-5
Cover illustration and interior art by Christine Finn

Suggestions for Use

The PIANO CAMP PRIMER LEVEL is designed especially for students who have had no piano study.

Having a piano camp for students before they begin lessons is an excellent way to give students a *head start* in learning some of the basic concepts taught in the first months of beginning lessons. Teaching these concepts in a group setting saves time for the teacher and student. In one hour teachers can teach a group of six students what would take six hours to teach individually. Students have fun with friends while learning. Games and competitions in the camp activities provide additional incentives to excel.

The PIANO CAMP PRIMER BOOK can be a tool for parents, teachers and students to evaluate the student's interest in music and to determine whether or not to continue lessons.

The concepts and activities in PIANO CAMP PRIMER LEVEL include those presented in ALFRED'S BASIC PIANO LIBRARY, Lesson Book 1A, through page 32.

This book may also be used in GROUP THEORY CLASSES during the year. It works equally well with other methods.

How to Schedule Piano Camps

Piano camps may be scheduled for the convenience of teachers and/or students.
The following are two of many options:

1. *Every day for one week,* meeting Monday through Friday for approximately two hours each session. (See illustration below of a teacher's schedule for groups of different levels.)

2. *Three times a week over a two week period,* meeting every Monday, Wednesday and Friday, OR meeting every Tuesday, Wednesday and Thursday for two hours each session. The Tuesday, Wednesday, Thursday schedule provides longer weekends for both teachers and students.

TEACHER'S WEEKLY PIANO CAMP SCHEDULE

Time *(Monday–Friday)*

8:00–10:00	GROUP ONE	*(Beginning Students)*
10:15–12:15	GROUP TWO	*(Early Elementary Students)*
Break for Lunch		
1:00–3:00	GROUP THREE	*(Elementary Students)*
3:15–5:15	GROUP FOUR	*(Late Elementary Students)*

A typical schedule for a two-hour session:

1. Use flash cards to review concepts to be taught in the session. (15 minutes)

2. Use note-reading, rhythm, music symbol, and keyboard activity pages from a session of the PIANO CAMP BOOK. Play at least one game contained in the book. (45 minutes)

3. Break for refreshments. (15 minutes)

4. Use remaining pages from the PIANO CAMP BOOK session.
   Play games as time permits.
   Give points and award prizes.
   Give assignments for the following day. (45 minutes)

Session 1

Finger Numbers

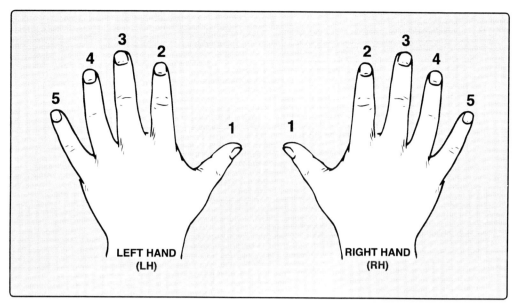

1. On each of the hands below, circle the indicated finger.

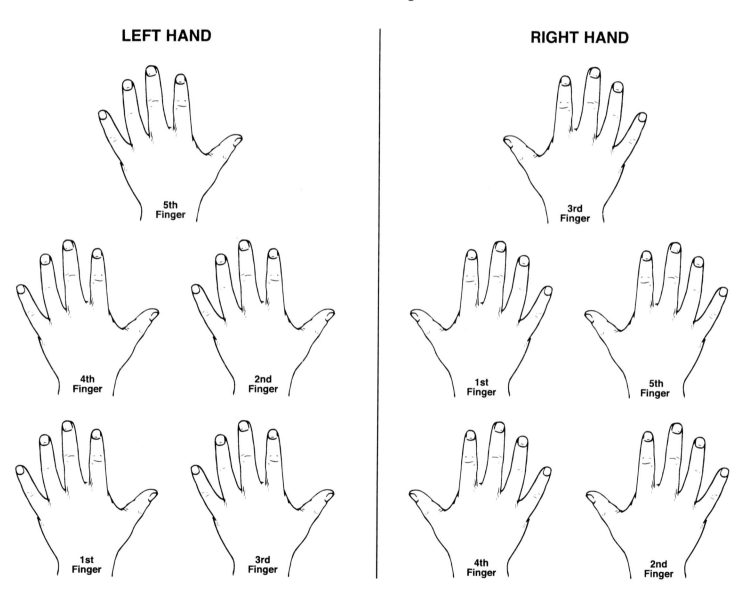

LEFT HAND   **RIGHT HAND**

5th Finger

3rd Finger

4th Finger   2nd Finger

1st Finger   5th Finger

1st Finger   3rd Finger

4th Finger   2nd Finger

2. Hold up both hands and wiggle both 1's, both 2's, both 3's, both 4's and both 5's.
   Your teacher will call out numbers of fingers for you to wiggle.

More Finger Numbers

1. Curve your fingers and tap the finger numbers in each example on a table top or any hard surface.
2. Say the finger numbers while you play.

1. LH

5 4 3 2 1 1 1

200 points

2. RH

1 2 3 4 5 5 5

200 points

3. LH

1 2 3 4 5 3 1

300 points

4. RH

2 3 4 5 3 2 1

400 points

5. LH

4 3 2 1 3 4 5

400 points

6. RH

5 4 3 2 1 3 5

300 points

NOTE TO TEACHER: A game may be made of this page by having students take turns rolling one die (or picking from 6 cards, numbered 1–6) and tapping the finger numbers in the example that matches the number rolled. If tapped correctly, the student receives the number of points printed in the box. If tapped incorrectly, play moves to the next student. The student with the most points after a specified period of time or number of turns is the winner.

Throughout the book, when the game star ⭐ is on the page, a game may be played by following the directions above.

Black Keys

The keyboard has white keys and black keys.
The black keys are in groups of 2's and 3's.

1. With a BROWN crayon, circle each group of 2 BLACK KEYS.

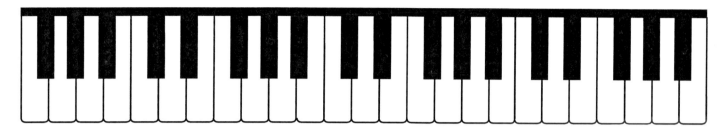

2. With an ORANGE crayon, circle each group of 3 BLACK KEYS.

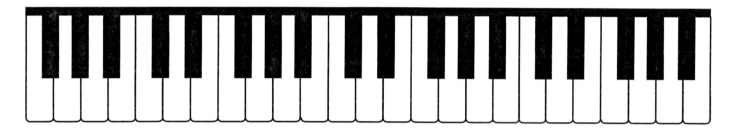

3. On the lines under the keyboard, write the number of BLACK KEYS
    in each group marked with an X. When you write the three numbers
    one after the other, you'll have the answer to the question!

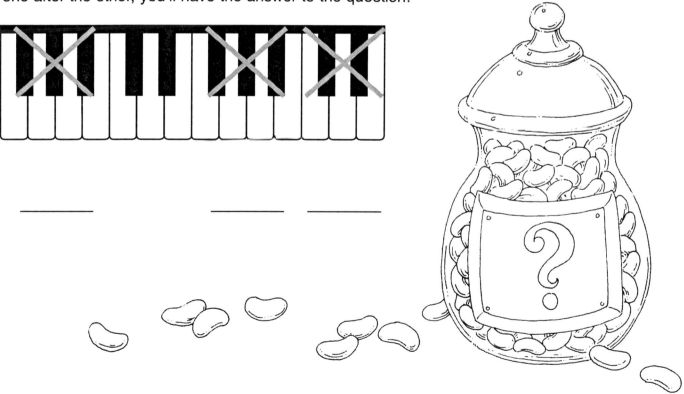

_____   _____   _____

How many jelly beans are in the jar? _____

Up and Down the Keyboard

1. Begin at the LOW end of the keyboard.
   Play groups of 2 BLACK KEYS, going *up* the keyboard (both keys at once).
   Listen to the sound as you play.

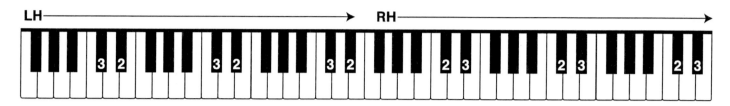

2. Begin at the HIGH end of the keyboard.
   Play groups of 3 BLACK KEYS, going *down* the keyboard (all 3 keys at once).
   Listen to the sound as you play.

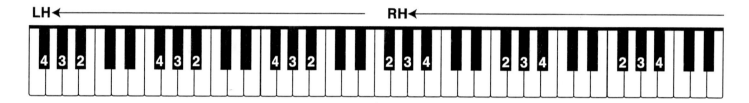

3. Color the circles with groups of 2 BLACK KEYS one color.
   Color the circles with groups of 3 BLACK KEYS a different color.

Quarter Note and Half Note

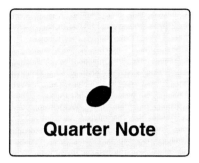

This is a QUARTER NOTE.
It receives 1 COUNT.

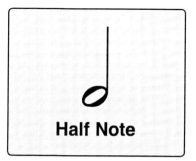

This is a HALF NOTE.
It receives 2 COUNTS.

1. Clap and count.

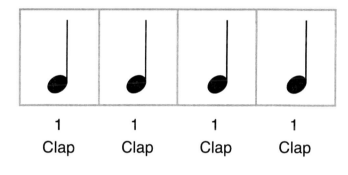

2. Draw a quarter note over each "1."

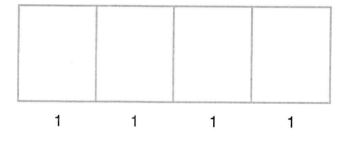

3. Clap and count.

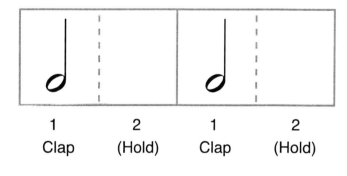

4. Draw a half note over each "1."

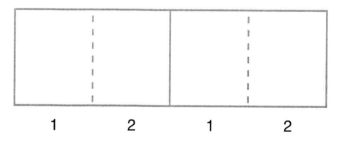

5. On the line below each note, write the number of counts the note receives.

Bar Lines, Repeat Sign

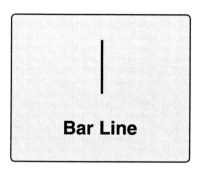

Bar Line

A BAR LINE divides
music into measures.

Double Bar

A DOUBLE BAR comes
at the end of a piece.

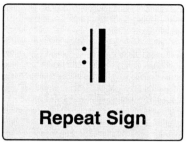

Repeat Sign

A REPEAT SIGN means to
go back to the beginning
and repeat the music.

1. Fill in the blanks.

    A _____ _____ comes at the end of a piece.

    A BAR LINE divides music into _____ .

    A REPEAT SIGN means to go back to the _____ and repeat the music.

2. Draw a BAR LINE after every TWO counts to divide these notes into measures.
   Draw a DOUBLE BAR at the end.

3. Draw a BAR LINE after every FOUR counts to divide these notes into measures.
   Draw a REPEAT SIGN at the end.

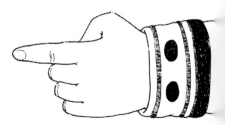

NOTE TO TEACHER: Play the game MUSIC POWER One on page 43. Follow the rules on page 42.

Clapping Rhythm Patterns

Clap these rhythm patterns while counting aloud.

GAME

1.

Count: 1   1   1   1   1   1   1   1

2.

Count: 1   2   1   2   1   2   1   2

3.

Count: 1   1   1   2   1   1   1   2

4.

Count: 1   2   1   1   1   2   1   1

5.

Count: 1   1   1   1   1   2   1   2

6.

Count: 1   2   1   2   1   1   1   1

WHEN PLAYING THE GAME:
Earn 200 points for each rhythm clapped correctly.

Music in Our Lives

Listen as your teacher reads these paragraphs about music in our lives.
Then fill in the blanks below.

*The world is filled with music. We can hear music in cars, doctors'
offices, banks, restaurants, and on TV and radio.*

*There are all kinds of music including classical, popular and jazz.
There are many kinds of concerts—school bands and choruses,
festivals, rock, folk, country, and sacred.*

*People all over the world like music. Music can be understood by
people in different countries, even though they speak different
languages. Music is sometimes called "the universal language."*

*Some music is very simple, like children's songs. Some music,
like a great symphony by Beethoven, is very complicated.*

*Music can make us feel sad or happy, lively or quiet, reverent or
mysterious. It can take us away from everyday life into a world of
happiness. It helps us enjoy our lives and do better work.*

1. List three places where you hear music each day.

   _____

   _____

   _____

2. What kind of music do you like to hear?

   _____

3. How can music make you feel better?

   _____

   _____

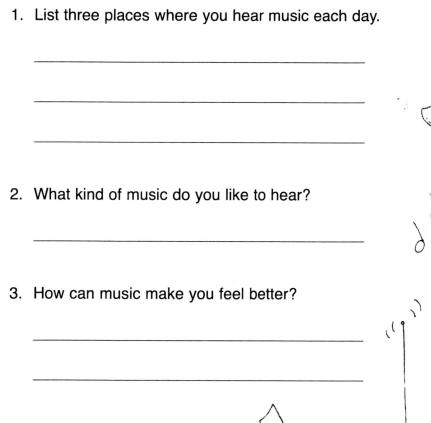

Session 2

The Music Alphabet

The white keys on the piano are named **A, B, C, D, E, F** and **G**— the first seven letters of the alphabet.

These letters are used over and over to name all the white keys.

1. Write the MUSIC ALPHABET in the squares on the keyboard. Begin with A.

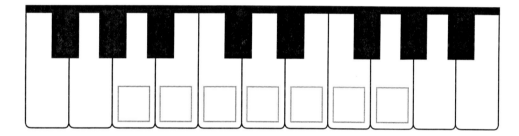

2. On the lines on the keys, write the letter names of the missing notes.

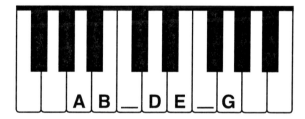

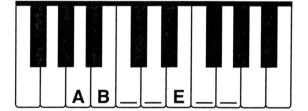

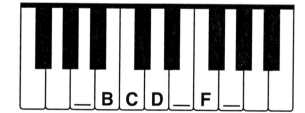

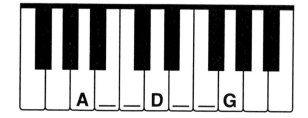

White Keys C~D~E

The white keys with the letter names C, D and E are located near the groups
of TWO BLACK KEYS.

C is the key to the LEFT of the two black keys.

D is BETWEEN the two black keys.

E is the key to the RIGHT of the two black keys.

1. On the keyboard below, find all of the C's. Print a C on each one.

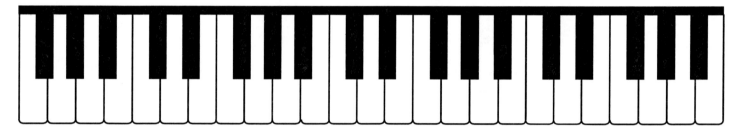

2. On the keyboard below, find all of the D's. Print a D on each one.

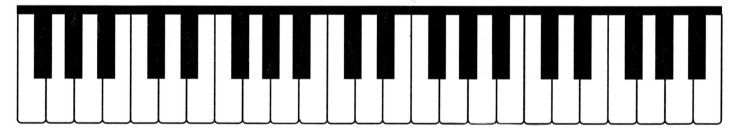

3. On the keyboard below, find all of the E's. Print an E on each one.

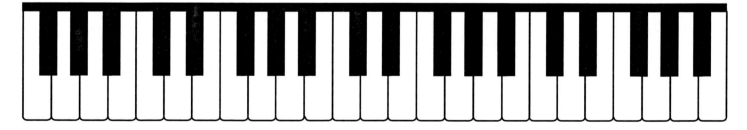

4. On the piano, find and play:

   A. All of the C's.

   B. All of the D's.

   C. All of the E's.

   D. All of the groups of C-D-E.

White Keys F-G-A-B

The white keys with the letter names F, G, A and B are located near the groups of THREE BLACK KEYS.

F is the key to the LEFT of the three black keys.

G is BETWEEN the 1st and 2nd of the three black keys.

A is BETWEEN the 2nd and 3rd of the three black keys.

B is the key to the RIGHT of the three black keys.

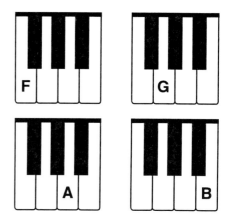

1. On the keyboard below, find all of the F's. Print an F on each one.

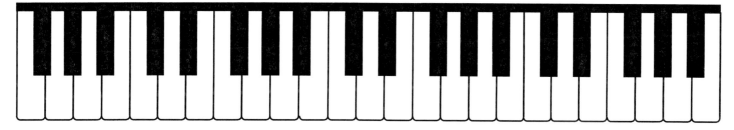

2. On the keyboard below, find all of the G's. Print a G on each one.

3. On the keyboard below, find all of the A's. Print an A on each one.

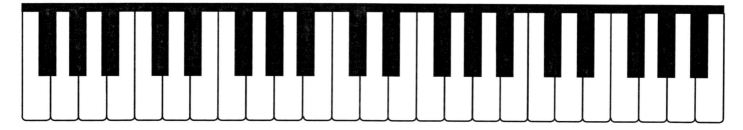

4. On the keyboard below, find all of the B's. Print a B on each one.

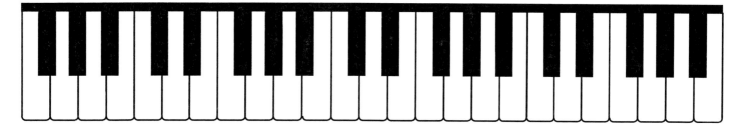

5. On the piano, find and play all of the F's, the G's, the A's, the B's and the groups of F-G-A-B.

Keyboard Activity

On the keyboard, find, name and play the indicated key or keys.

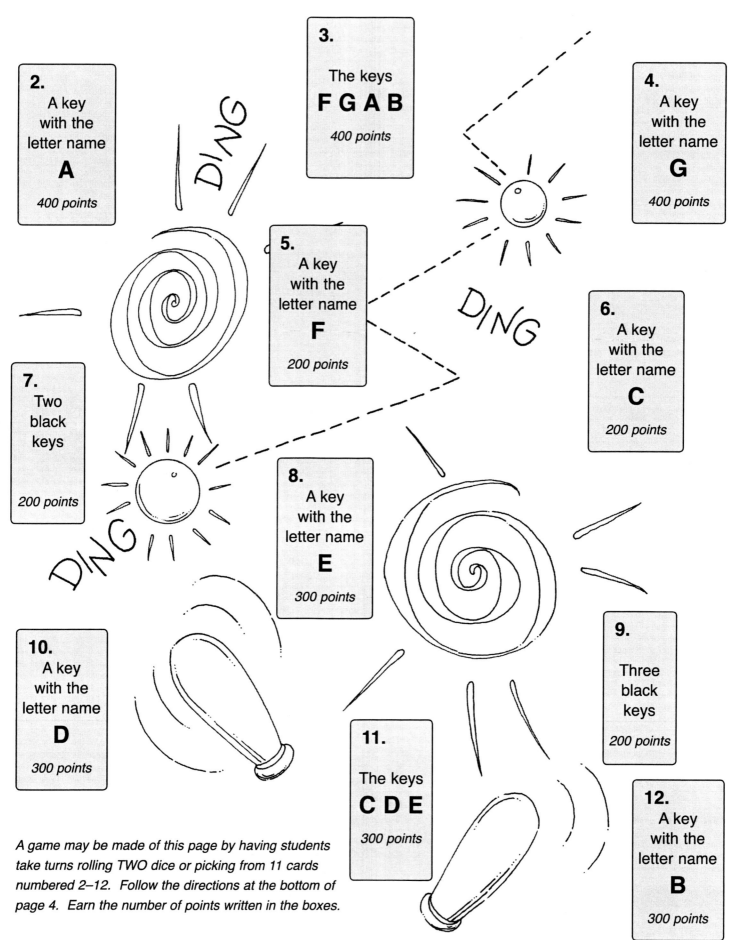

2.
A key with the letter name
A
400 points

3.
The keys
F G A B
400 points

4.
A key with the letter name
G
400 points

5.
A key with the letter name
F
200 points

6.
A key with the letter name
C
200 points

7.
Two black keys
200 points

8.
A key with the letter name
E
300 points

9.
Three black keys
200 points

10.
A key with the letter name
D
300 points

11.
The keys
C D E
300 points

12.
A key with the letter name
B
300 points

A game may be made of this page by having students take turns rolling TWO dice or picking from 11 cards numbered 2–12. Follow the directions at the bottom of page 4. Earn the number of points written in the boxes.

Piano (*p*) and Forte (*f*)

DYNAMIC SIGNS tell us how SOFTLY or LOUDLY to play.

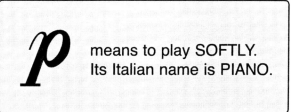

p means to play SOFTLY.
Its Italian name is PIANO.

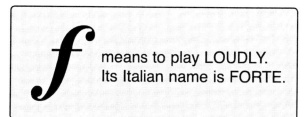

f means to play LOUDLY.
Its Italian name is FORTE.

1. Trace the dynamic sign that means to play SOFTLY. Draw three more.

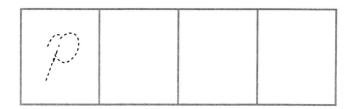

2. Trace the dynamic sign that means to play LOUDLY. Draw three more.

3. Using the rhythm and words given below, create a melody using a group of 3 black keys. Begin and end with the fingerings given. Use HIGH tones, playing SOFTLY with the right hand.

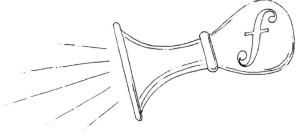

Ssh! Please be   qui - et!   Don't wake up   the   ba - by!

4. Using the rhythm and words given below, create a melody using a group of 3 black keys. Begin and end with the fingerings given. Use LOW tones, playing LOUDLY with the left hand.

Come and hear the   march-ing band! It's   ver - y   loud and   ver - y grand!

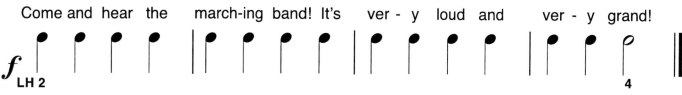

NOTE TO TEACHER: Select the question cards numbered 1–16 plus the "Free Space" cards from page 47. Using the gameboard on page 45, play the MUSIC RACE GAME. Follow the rules for play on page 42.

Listening

Your teacher will clap ONE of the rhythm patterns in each box.
Circle the pattern that you hear.

Music Symbol Match

On each line below, write the letter name of the box that contains the matching musical symbol.

a.

b.

c.

d.

e.

f.

g.

h.

BAR LINE_____

HALF NOTE _____

DOUBLE BAR_____

REPEAT SIGN_____

QUARTER NOTE_____

TWO BLACK KEYS_____

MEASURE_____

THREE BLACK KEYS_____

*NOTE TO TEACHER: Play the game
MUSIC POWER One on page 43.
Follow the rules on page 42.*

How Music Began

Listen as your teacher reads these paragraphs about how music began.
Complete the sentences by unscrambling the letters and filling in the blanks.

Primitive men and women were primarily hunters who lived in shelters and caves. The very first music came from their voices and bodies.

As they listened to the sounds of nature around them (the birds' songs, the rhythmic beating of the rain, wind whistling through the trees, the babbling of water in a stream, the thunder and lightning in a storm) they imitated these sounds with their voices.

They shrieked, howled, wailed, whistled, hummed, hissed and clicked to make sounds. They clapped, stamped, jumped and slapped their bodies to the beat as they danced.

They hunted to have food to eat, but they were also adventurers and artists. There are no written words to tell us about their lives, but we can learn much from primitive paintings drawn on the walls of the caves where they lived.

They probably used music as they worked making shelters, chipping stones to make drills, knives and spear points, and preparing food. They communicated with others through music and dance. Ceremonial music and dance strengthened the bonds of their families and their tribes as they performed together.

1. Primitive men and women first made music

   with their (COSVIE)_____ and bodies.

2. They responded to and imitated the sounds they heard

   in (TARNUE)_____.

3. We can learn about primitive music from

   (GAPSINNIT)_____ drawn on the walls of caves.

Session 3

Naming White Keys—Story

Name the keys marked with an X. Fill in the
blanks under the keyboards to complete the story.

Clara the Parakeet

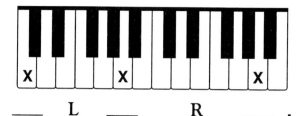

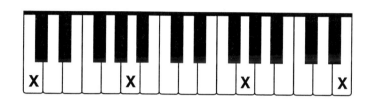

Once there was a parakeet named ___ L ___ R ___ .

She had a beautiful ___ ___ ___ ___ that was

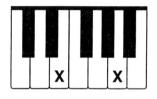

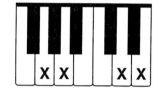

N ___ ___ R a window so she could see the lovely ___ ___ R ___ ___ N.

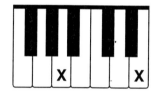

She was owned by three pretty girls, ___ N N ___ ,

M ___ R Y ___ ___ T H, and H ___ N N ___ H.

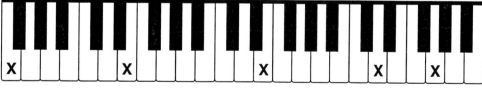

They took turns ___ ___ ___ ___ I N ___ her.

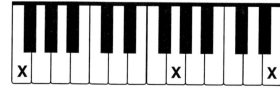

Sometimes she would sit on one of their ___ I N ___ ___ R S

and chirp a lovely song.

Middle C Position

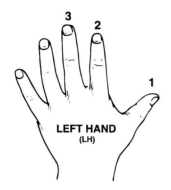

LEFT HAND
(LH)

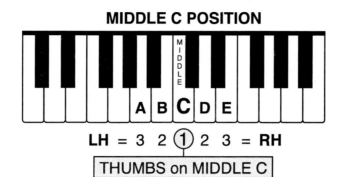

MIDDLE C POSITION

A B C D E

LH = 3 2 ① 2 3 = RH

THUMBS on MIDDLE C

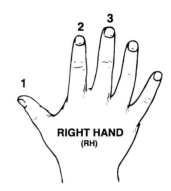

RIGHT HAND
(RH)

PRACTICE DIRECTIONS:

1. Clap (or tap) and count aloud.
2. Say finger numbers aloud while playing them in the air.
3. Play and count aloud.
4. Play and say note names.
5. Play and sing the words.

Practice each new piece following these steps.

Yankee Doodle

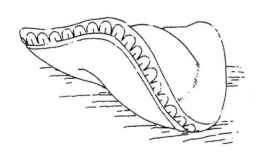

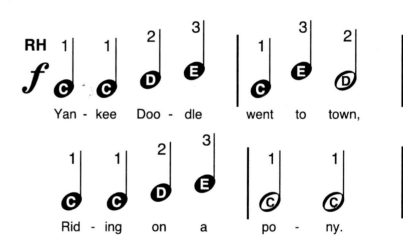

RH

Yan - kee Doo - dle went to town,

Rid - ing on a po - ny.

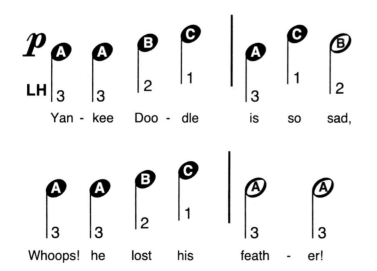

Yan - kee Doo - dle is so sad,

Whoops! he lost his feath - er!

Sight Reading

PRACTICE DIRECTIONS:

- Clap and count aloud.
- Say letter names.
- Play slowly while saying letter names.

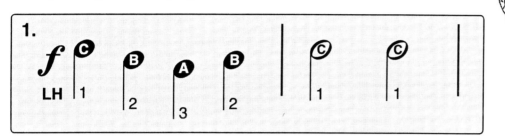

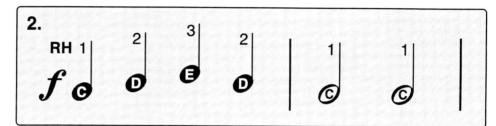

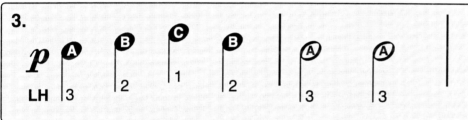

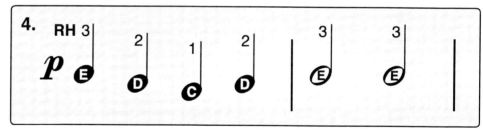

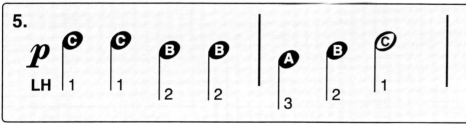

WHEN PLAYING THE GAME:

Earn 100 points for playing with a strong even beat, counting aloud.
Earn 100 points for playing the notes correctly.

Whole Note

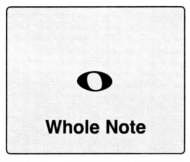

Whole Note

This is a WHOLE NOTE.
It receives 4 COUNTS.

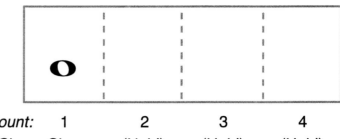

Count: 1   2   3   4
Clap: Clap   (Hold)   (Hold)   (Hold)

1. Draw a WHOLE NOTE over each "1." Clap and count.

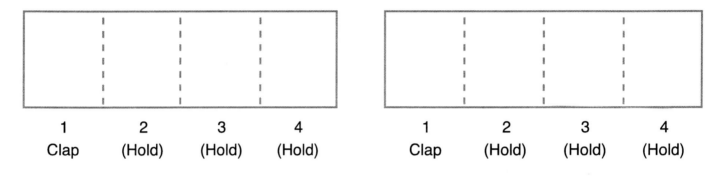

1	2	3	4
Clap	(Hold)	(Hold)	(Hold)

1	2	3	4
Clap	(Hold)	(Hold)	(Hold)

2. Clap these rhythms, counting aloud.

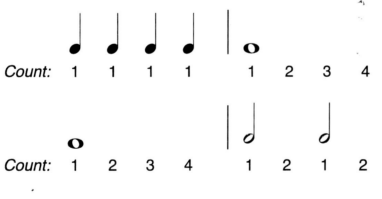

Count: 1   1   1   1   1   2   3   4

Count: 1   2   3   4   1   2   1   2

3. With a RED crayon, circle the QUARTER NOTES.
   With a GREEN crayon, circle the HALF NOTES.
   With a BLUE crayon, circle the WHOLE NOTES.

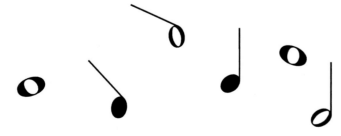

*NOTE TO TEACHER: Select the question cards numbered 1–17 and the "Free Space" cards from page 47.
Using the game board on page 45, play the MUSIC RACE game.*

Time Signature 𝄴⁴⁄₄

At the beginning of a piece of music there are two numbers called the TIME SIGNATURE.

The **TOP NUMBER** tells the NUMBER OF COUNTS in each measure.   **4**   Four counts in each measure.

The **BOTTOM NUMBER** tells what KIND OF NOTE receives ONE count.   **4**   A quarter note ♩ gets one count.

1. Draw a 𝟐⁄₄ time signature three times. _____ _____ _____

2. Complete these measures with ONE note to equal FOUR counts in each measure.

    ⁴⁄₄ ♩ ♩ ♩ ___ | 𝅗𝅥 ___ | 𝅝 ‖

3. Complete these measures with TWO notes to equal FOUR counts in each measure.

    ⁴⁄₄ ♩ ___ ___ | ___ ___ 𝅗𝅥 ‖

4. Draw a line from each symbol to its matching name.

- TIME SIGNATURE

- QUARTER NOTE

- WHOLE NOTE

- HALF NOTE

Middle C Position

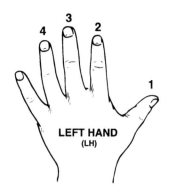

LEFT HAND
(LH)

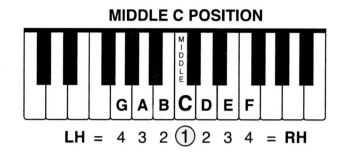

MIDDLE C POSITION

G A B **C** D E F

LH = 4 3 2 ① 2 3 4 = RH

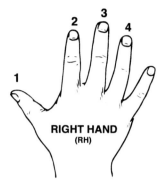

RIGHT HAND
(RH)

PRACTICE DIRECTIONS:

1. Clap (or tap) and count aloud.

2. Say finger numbers aloud while playing them in the air.

3. Play and count aloud.

4. Play and say note names.

5. Play and sing the words.

Practice each new piece following these steps.

Wedding Bells

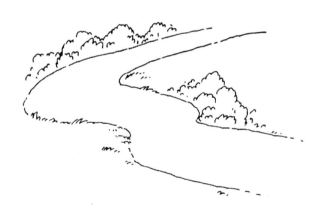

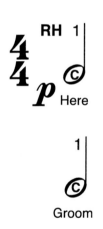

$\frac{4}{4}$ RH 1

p ©
Here

4
F
comes

4
F
the

4
F
bride.

1
©
Groom

2
D
by

3
E
her

4
F
side.

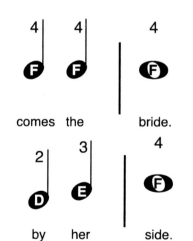

p
Wed -
©
LH 4

ding
C
1

bells
C
1

sound
C
1

All
©
4

through
A
3

the
B
2

town!
C
1

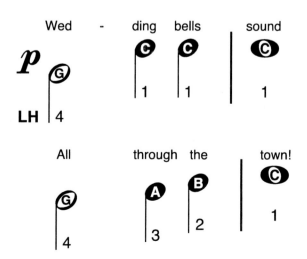

Sight Reading

PRACTICE DIRECTIONS:

- Clap and count aloud.
- Say letter names.
- Play slowly while saying letter names.

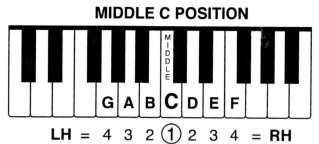

MIDDLE C POSITION

LH = 4 3 2 ① 2 3 4 = RH

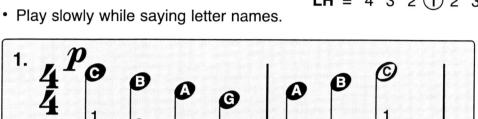

1.

2.

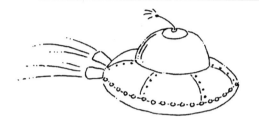

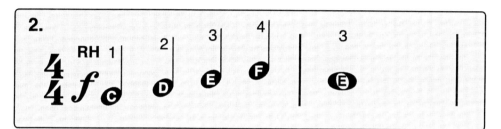

3.

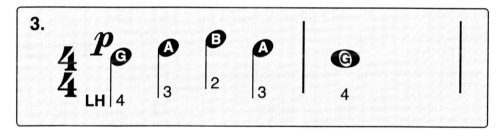

4.

5.

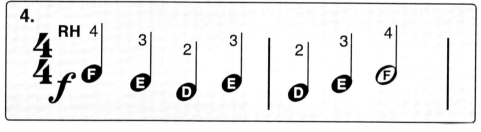

6.

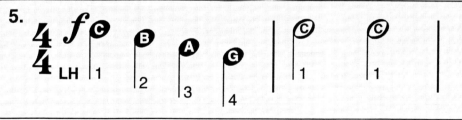

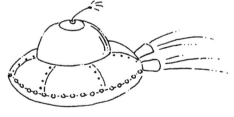

WHEN PLAYING THE GAME:

Earn 100 points for playing with a strong even beat, counting aloud.
Earn 100 points for playing the notes correctly.

Primitive Instruments

Listen as your teacher reads these paragraphs about how music began. Fill in the blanks to complete the sentence below, then find and circle the words in the word search box.

As primitive men and women advanced, they found that they could make music using other things besides their voices and bodies. They found that if they added instruments to their voices, the music was more impressive. They began to make instruments out of materials that were around them.

WHISTLES and FLUTES were made from wood, hollow-stemmed reeds, corn stalks, clay or bone. Reed flutes were made by scraping out the center of the reed, splitting the reed lengthwise, boring the holes, sealing with adhesive, then securing with strips of leather around it.

DRUMS varied in size from small hand drums to drums large enough for many drummers to sit around. They were made from logs, hoops, bowls or baskets covered with animal hide. Often they were decorated with native paint, feathers, fur or beads.

RATTLES and SCRAPERS were considered sacred and usually were used only in special rituals. Small hard objects (stones or hard clay balls) were put in containers such as gourds or turtle shells to make rattles. Notches were carved in wood or bone and a stick was rubbed across the notches to make scrapers.

These early instruments were the primitive versions of the instruments that we use today.

Among the kinds of instruments made by primitive people were the

_____, _____, _____, _____ and _____.

W	L	R	A	T	T	L	E
A	H	Q	B	F	K	M	D
D	N	I	P	L	X	S	Y
R	I	F	S	U	P	H	S
U	W	M	Z	T	B	A	R
M	G	J	N	E	L	H	G
F	S	C	R	A	P	E	R
T	D	O	X	N	B	Y	C

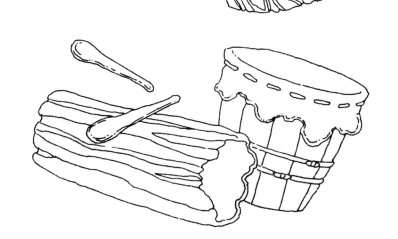

Session 4

Middle C Position

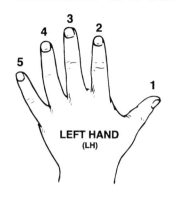

LEFT HAND
(LH)

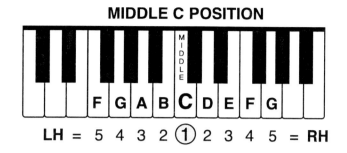

MIDDLE C POSITION

F G A B **C** D E F G

LH = 5 4 3 2 ① 2 3 4 5 = RH

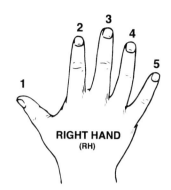

RIGHT HAND
(RH)

PRACTICE DIRECTIONS:

1. Clap (or tap) and count aloud.

2. Say finger numbers aloud while playing them in the air.

3. Play and count aloud.

4. Play and say note names.

5. Play and sing the words.

Practice each new piece following these steps.

Jingle Bells

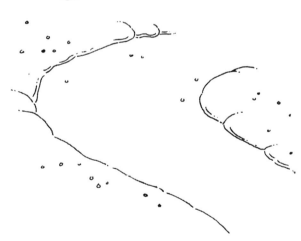

RH

4/4 f

3 | E   3 | E   3 | E | 3 | E   3 | E   3 | E |

Jin - gle   bells,   Jin - gle   bells,

3 | E   5 | G   1 | C   2 | D | 3 | E |

Jin - gle   all   the   way.

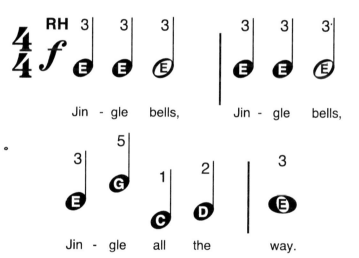

LH

f

Jin - gle   bells,   Jin - gle   bells,

F | 5   F | 5   F | 5 | F | 5   F | 5   F | 5 |

One   horse   o - pen   sleigh!

G | 4   G | 4   A | 3   B | 2 | C | 1 |

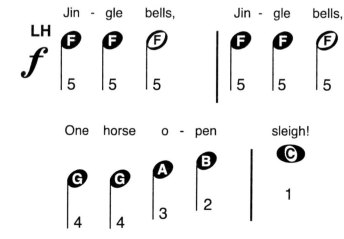

28

Sight Reading

PRACTICE DIRECTIONS:

- Clap and count aloud.
- Say letter names.
- Play slowly while saying letter names.

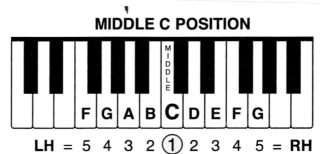

MIDDLE C POSITION

F G A B **C** D E F G

LH = 5 4 3 2 ① 2 3 4 5 = RH

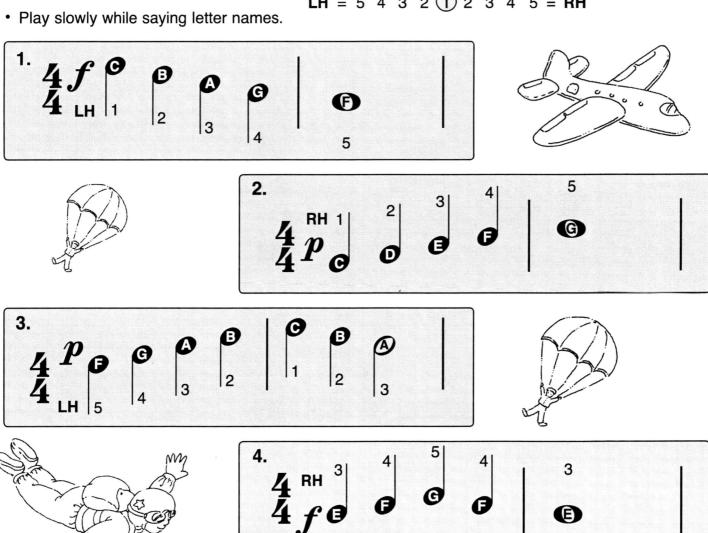

1.
4/4 *f* LH C(1) B(2) A(3) G(4) | F(5) |

2.
4/4 RH *p* C(1) D(2) E(3) F(4) | G(5) |

3.
4/4 *p* LH F(5) G(4) A(3) B(2) | C(1) B(2) A(3) |

4.
4/4 RH *f* E(3) F(4) G(5) F(4) | E(3) |

5.
4/4 *p* LH A(3) G(4) F(5) G(4) | A(3) B(2) C(1) |

6.
4/4 RH *f* G(5) F(4) E(3) F(4) | G(5) F(4) E(3) |

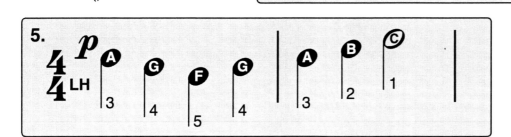

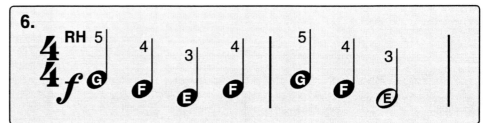

WHEN PLAYING THE GAME:

Earn 100 points for playing with a strong even beat, counting aloud.
Earn 100 points for playing the notes correctly.

Time Signature $\frac{3}{4}$ and Dotted Half Note

TIME SIGNATURE

$\frac{3}{4}$ means **3** beats to each measure.

a **QUARTER NOTE** gets **1** beat.

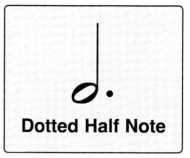

Dotted Half Note

This is a DOTTED HALF NOTE.
It receives 3 COUNTS.

1. Clap and count.

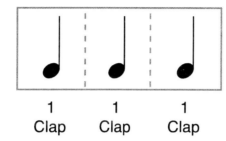

1	1	1
Clap	Clap	Clap

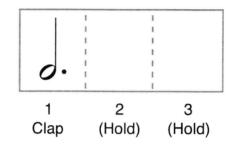

1	2	3
Clap	(Hold)	(Hold)

2. Draw a DOTTED HALF NOTE over each "1."

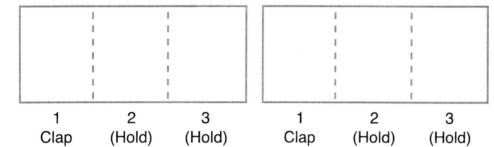

1	2	3		1	2	3		1	2	3
Clap	(Hold)	(Hold)		Clap	(Hold)	(Hold)		Clap	(Hold)	(Hold)

3. Clap this rhythm while counting aloud.

4. With a RED crayon, circle the QUARTER NOTES.
   With a GREEN crayon, circle the HALF NOTES.
   With a BLUE crayon, circle the WHOLE NOTES.
   With an ORANGE crayon, circle the DOTTED HALF NOTES.

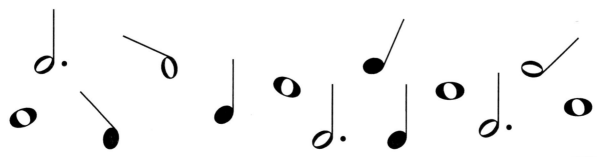

SESSION 4

Crossword Puzzle—Music Symbols

Complete the sentences below, then solve the crossword puzzle.
Choose answers from the given words.

Repeat

Softly

Loudly

Half

Three

Whole

Signature

Quarter

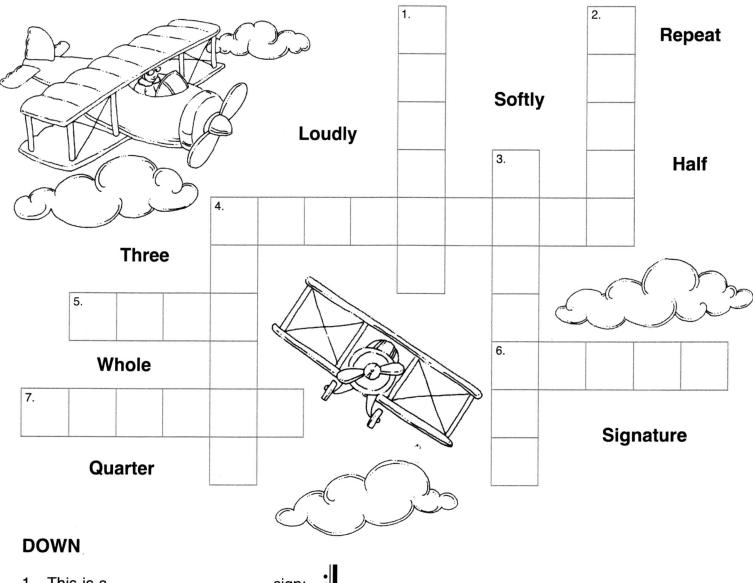

DOWN

1. This is a _____ sign: :‖

2. A _____ note (𝐎) receives 4 counts in 4/4 time.

3. This is a _____ note: ♩

4. The symbol *p* means to play _____ .

ACROSS

4. This is called a time _____ : 4/4

5. A _____ note (♩) receives 2 counts in 4/4 time.

6. A dotted half note (♩.) receives _____ counts in 4/4 time.

7. The symbol *f* means to play _____ .

NOTE TO TEACHER: Play the game
MUSIC POWER One on page 43.
Follow the rules on page 42.

C Position

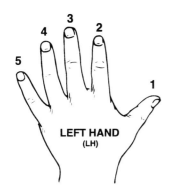

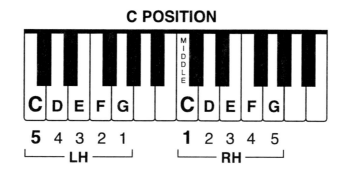

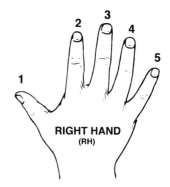

PRACTICE DIRECTIONS:

1. Clap (or tap) and count aloud.

2. Say finger numbers aloud while playing them in the air.

3. Play and count aloud.

4. Play and say note names.

5. Play and sing the words.

Practice each new piece following these steps.

Song of Joy

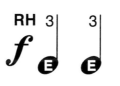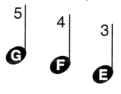
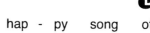

Come and sing a hap - py song of

joy for peo - ple ev - 'ry - where,

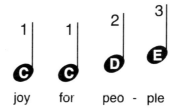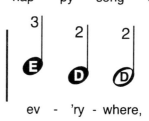

Sing a song of peace and love for

all the na - tions far and near.

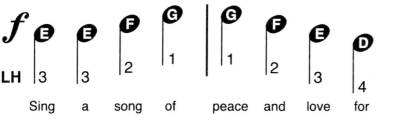

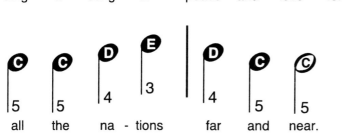

Sight Reading

PRACTICE DIRECTIONS:

- Clap and count aloud.
- Say letter names.
- Play slowly while saying letter names.

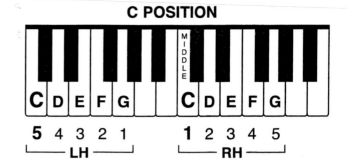

C POSITION

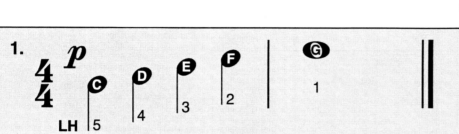

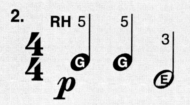

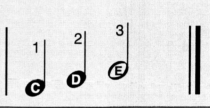

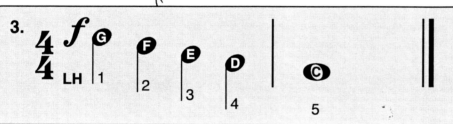

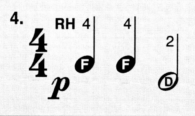

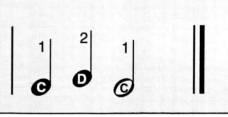

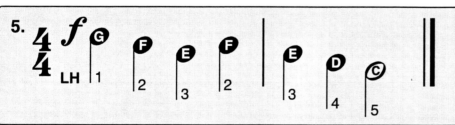

WHEN PLAYING THE GAME:

Earn 100 points for playing with a strong even beat, counting aloud.

Earn 100 points for playing the notes correctly.

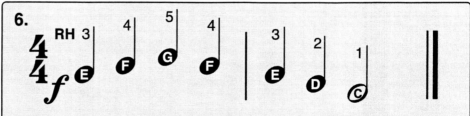

Listening

Your teacher will play ONE of the examples in each box.
Circle the example that you hear.

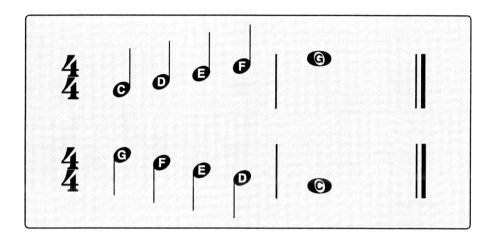

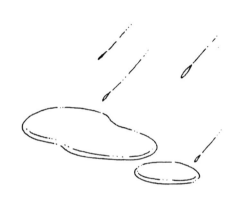

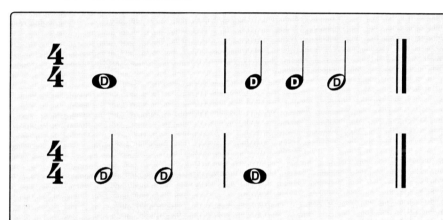

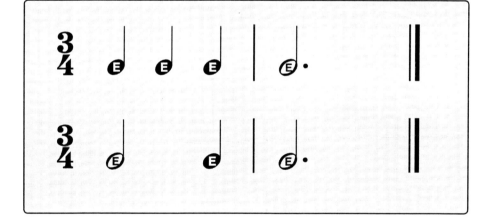

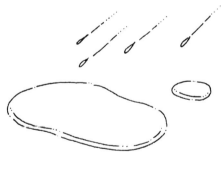

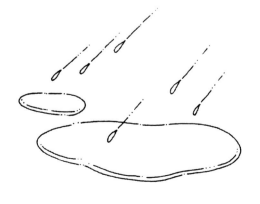

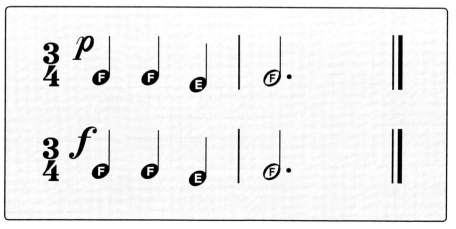

Music in Ancient Civilizations

Listen as your teacher reads these paragraphs about music in ancient civilizations.
Using the words in the box, fill in the sentences below.

By the time the first great civilizations had developed in the Ancient World, a large number of instruments had been developed and refined.

In EGYPT, flutes and sistra (a kind of rattle) were used in temple ceremonies. Egyptians were largely responsible for the development of the lyre and harp family of instruments.

It is from the ancient GREEK civilization that we get the word music. *"Mousike" was named for the muses, the goddesses of inspiration. The Greeks developed ways to organize music into scales.*

ORIENTAL music used the 5-tone (pentatonic) scale. An easy way to play this scale is to play the black keys of the piano.

HEBREW music and instruments are mentioned numerous times in the Bible. Psalm 150 says:

> *Praise him with trumpet sound;*
> > *Praise him with lute and harp!*
> *Praise him with timbrel and dance;*
> > *Praise him with strings and pipe!*
> *Praise him with sounding cymbals;*
> > *Praise him with loud clashing cymbals!*

The ROMANS used music in their dramatic plays. Gladiator fights were accompanied by trumpets and cymbals. Later in Italy, a system for writing music was developed.

From the beginning, music has been used in worship, work and play.

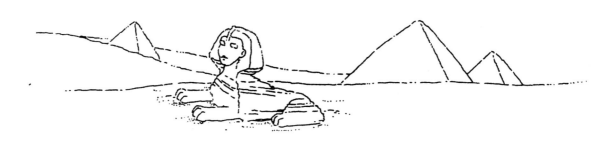

1. _____ music uses the 5-tone scale.

2. The _____ were largely responsible for the development of the lyre and harp family.

3. We learn much about _____ music from the Bible.

4. It is from the _____ civilization that we get the word *music.*

5. The _____ used trumpets and cymbals to accompany gladiator fights.

| GREEK |
| ROMANS |
| HEBREW |
| ORIENTAL |
| EGYPTIANS |

Session 5

The Staff

Music is written on a staff that has 5 LINES and 4 SPACES.

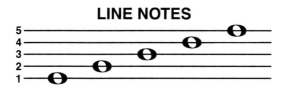

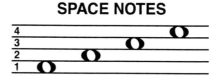

1. Trace the dotted lines to make a line note. Draw two more whole notes on the line.

2. Trace the dotted lines to make a space note. Draw two more whole notes in the space.

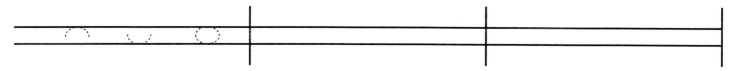

3. Draw a note on each line.

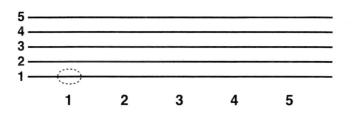

    1   2   3   4   5

4. Draw a note in each space.

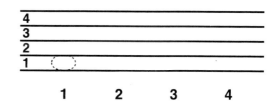

    1   2   3   4

5. Circle the word "line" for line notes or "space" for space notes.

line	line	line	line	line	line	line	line
space	space	space	space	space	space	space	space

6. On the staff, draw the indicated notes. Remember to count lines or spaces from the bottom to the top.

3rd space	4th line	5th line	2nd line	1st line	3rd line	2nd space	4th space

Bass Clef Sign

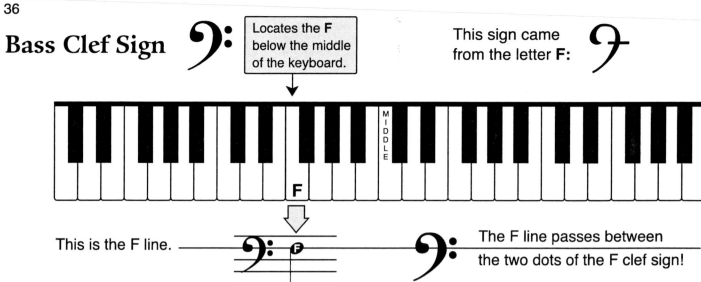

Trace the dotted lines to draw a bass clef sign. Draw four more.

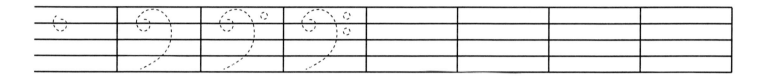

Treble Clef Sign

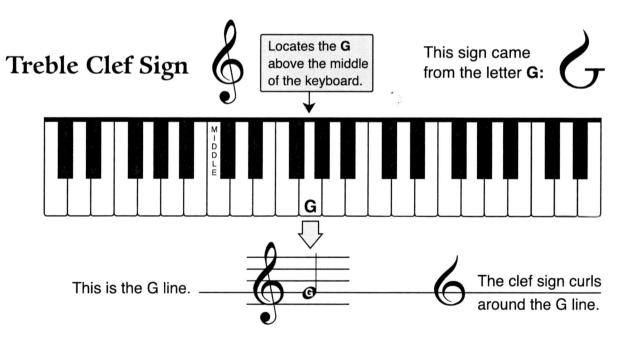

Trace the dotted lines to draw a treble clef sign. Draw four more.

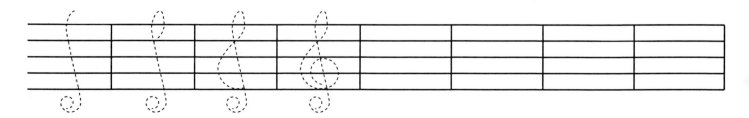

NOTE TO TEACHER: Play the game MUSIC POWER Two on page 44. Follow the rules on page 42.

C Position—Bass Staff

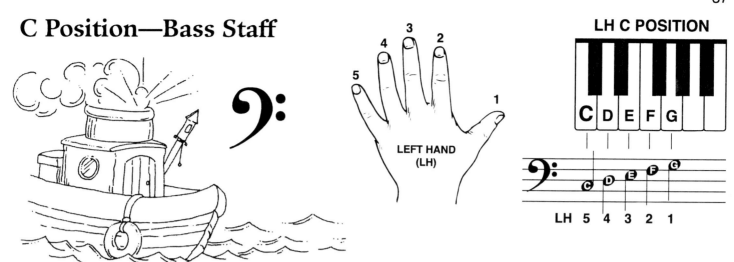

LEFT HAND (LH)

LH C POSITION

LH 5 4 3 2 1

Play the following exercises, saying the words as you play.

1

LH 1

Fourth space G with fin-ger 1, the next note down is F.

2

LH 2

Fourth line F with fin-ger 2, the next note down is E.

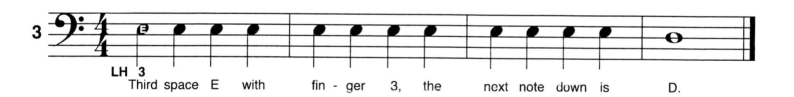

3

LH 3

Third space E with fin-ger 3, the next note down is D.

4

LH 4

Third line D with fin-ger 4, the next note down is C.

5

LH 5

C's with 5, then up we go, C, D, E, F, G.

C Position—Treble Staff

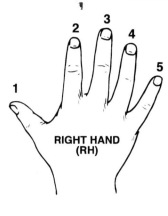
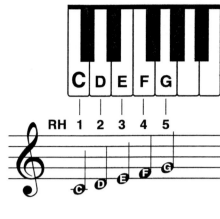

RH C POSITION

Play the following exercises, saying the words as you play.

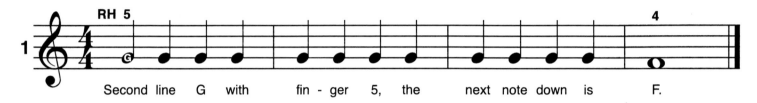

1. Second line G with fin-ger 5, the next note down is F.

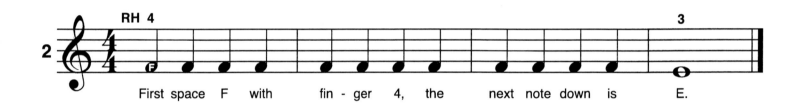

2. First space F with fin-ger 4, the next note down is E.

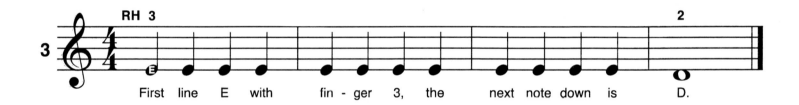

3. First line E with fin-ger 3, the next note down is D.

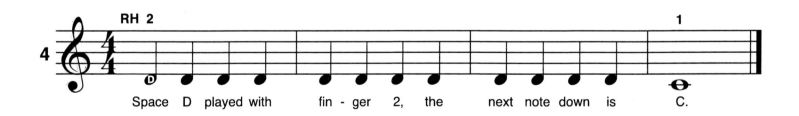

4. Space D played with fin-ger 2, the next note down is C.

5. This note is called Mid-dle C. C, D, E, F, G.

The Grand Staff

The TREBLE STAFF and BASS STAFF together make the GRAND STAFF. A short line is used between them for MIDDLE C.

A BRACE and BAR LINE join the staves.
A DOUBLE BAR comes at the end of a piece.

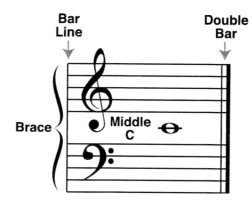

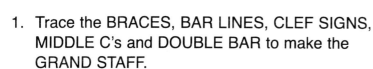

1. Trace the BRACES, BAR LINES, CLEF SIGNS, MIDDLE C's and DOUBLE BAR to make the GRAND STAFF.

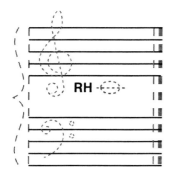 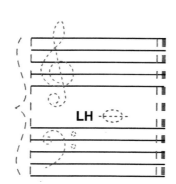

2. Draw the GRAND STAFF two times.

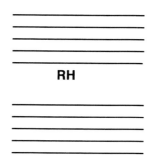 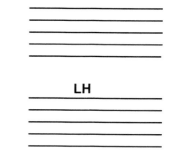

3. On the keyboard, draw the letter names of the keys, beginning with the lowest A and ending with the highest G. (You will use the complete MUSICAL ALPHABET 3 times.)

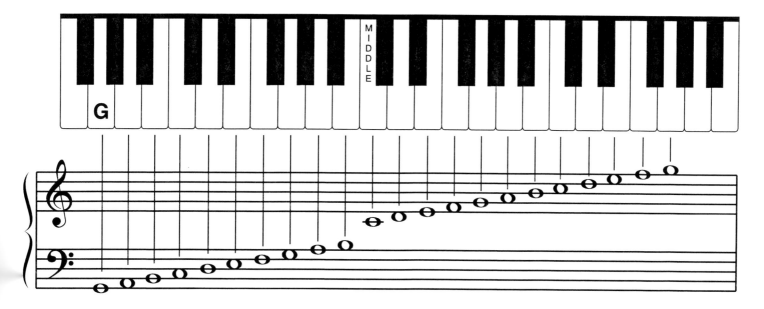

4. On the keyboard and staff above, circle the keys and notes of the C POSITION.

General Review

Draw the indicated note or symbol.

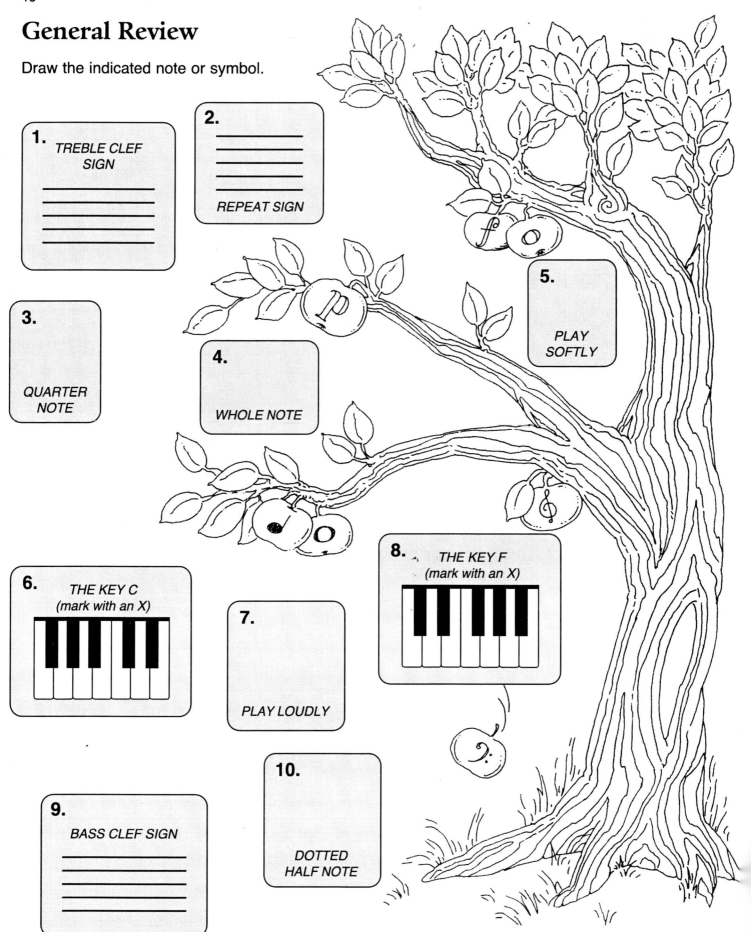

1. TREBLE CLEF SIGN

2. REPEAT SIGN

3. QUARTER NOTE

4. WHOLE NOTE

5. PLAY SOFTLY

6. THE KEY C (mark with an X)

7. PLAY LOUDLY

8. THE KEY F (mark with an X)

9. BASS CLEF SIGN

10. DOTTED HALF NOTE

NOTE TO TEACHER: Using all of the question cards from page 47 and the game board on page 45, play the MUSIC RACE GAME. Follow the rules for play on page 42.

The Development of Keyboard Instruments

Listen as your teacher reads these paragraphs about the development of keyboard instruments. Fill in the blanks to complete the sentences below, then find and circle the words in the word search box.

The first keyboard instrument was the ORGAN. The organ has different sized pipes that produce different sounds. The large pipes produce the lower tones, while the small pipes produce the higher tones. In the span of several hundred years, the organ progressed from the simple hand-held organ called the "positive," to the very ornate organ of the Baroque period (1600–1750).

Another of the early keyboard instruments was the CLAVICHORD, a small instrument that was used most often in the home for practice and entertainment. The sound was made by a small brass tangent which would strike the strings. A soft, delicate sound was made when the keys were depressed.

The HARPSICHORD became a very important instrument. It was played for pleasure and entertainment in homes, but it was also used in concerts. A quill plucked the strings when a key was depressed. The sound of the harpsichord is delicate (guitar-like), but louder than the clavichord.

The FORTEPIANO was the forerunner of the modern piano. It could be played loudly (forte) and softly (piano) by the degree of strength used in depressing the keys. Bartolommeo Cristofori, an Italian, invented the first piano in about 1709. The strings are struck by felt hammers when the keys are depressed, making a stronger, more melodious tone.

B	F	I	L	C	V	Q	D
C	O	N	C	E	R	T	S
X	R	T	S	U	J	Y	P
H	G	M	P	I	A	N	O
T	A	N	G	E	N	T	K
K	N	O	R	W	G	Z	M

1. The first keyboard instrument was the _____.

2. The harpsichord was used in _____ as well as in homes.

3. The first _____ was made by Bartolommeo Cristofori.

4. The sounds of a clavichord were made by a _____ striking the strings.

Games

Rules for Play

MUSIC POWER One and Two

(Either one of the dice or 6 small cards numbered 1–6 are needed for MUSIC POWER One. Either a pair of dice or 11 small cards numbered 2–12 are needed for MUSIC POWER Two.)

Students take turns rolling the dice (or drawing a card). Each student must identify the symbol that matches the number he/she rolls (or draws). If the student answers correctly, he/she receives the number of points written in the symbol box. If incorrect, he/she receives no points and the turn moves to the next player. That player may then name the symbol just missed by the previous player or choose to roll himself/herself.

Keep playing until all students have had a designated number of turns. (The number of turns will depend on how many students are playing and the time schedule.) If a player rolls or draws the same number more than once, he may elect to roll again or name the symbol again. Keep a record of points. The student with the most points wins.

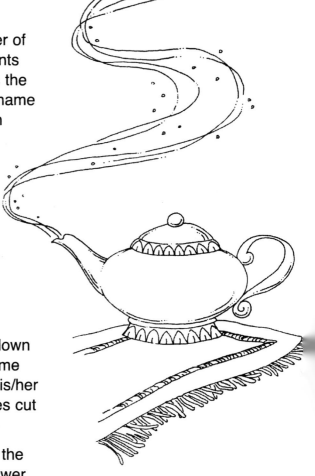

MUSIC POWER One
1. quarter note (1 count)
2. double bar
3. a measure
4. half note (2 counts)
5. repeat sign
6. bar line

MUSIC POWER Two
2. time signature
3. whole note (4 counts)
4. forte (loud)
5. dotted half note (3 counts)
6. note on a line
7. white keys CDE

8. piano (soft)
9. treble clef sign
10. bass clef sign
11. note in a space
12. white keys FGAB

MUSIC RACE

Question cards (p. 47) should be cut apart and placed face down randomly on the table. Each student will use his/her own game board (p. 45). Each student will also need a token to mark his/her place. Coins, buttons, tokens from old games, or small circles cut from construction paper may be used for tokens.

Students take turns drawing a card and placing it face up on the table. If the student can fill in the blanks with the correct answer, he/she may move forward on the board the number of spaces listed on the card. If the student does not name the note correctly, he/she then remains on the same space and the turn goes to the next player. If a student draws a "Free Space" card, he/she moves the number of spaces listed on the card without having to answer a question. The student who moves enough or more than enough spaces to land on the winning circle wins.

MUSIC RACE

1. two	5. double bar	9. D	13. A	17. whole
2. three	6. repeat	10. E	14. B	18. time signature
3. quarter	7. music	11. F	15. softly	19. dotted half
4. half	8. C	12. G	16. loudly	20. treble
				21. bass

SUGGESTION TO TEACHER: To make the game boards and question cards last longer, they may be removed from the book and laminated.

MUSIC POWER One

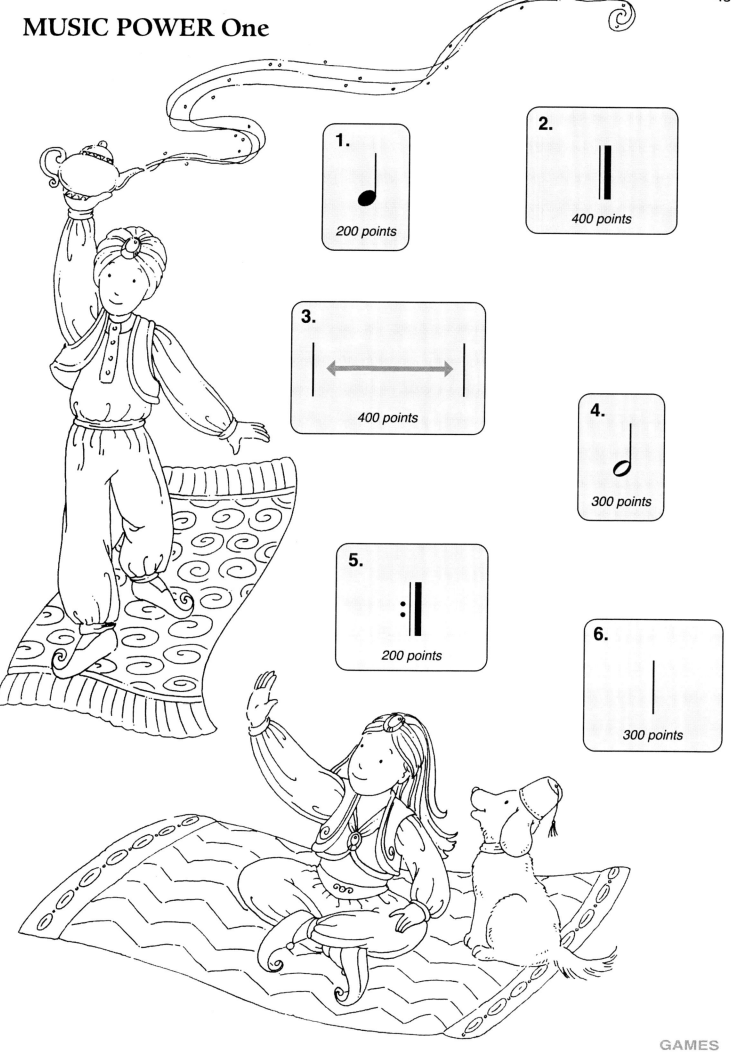

1.
200 points

2.
400 points

3.
400 points

4.
300 points

5.
200 points

6.
300 points

MUSIC POWER Two

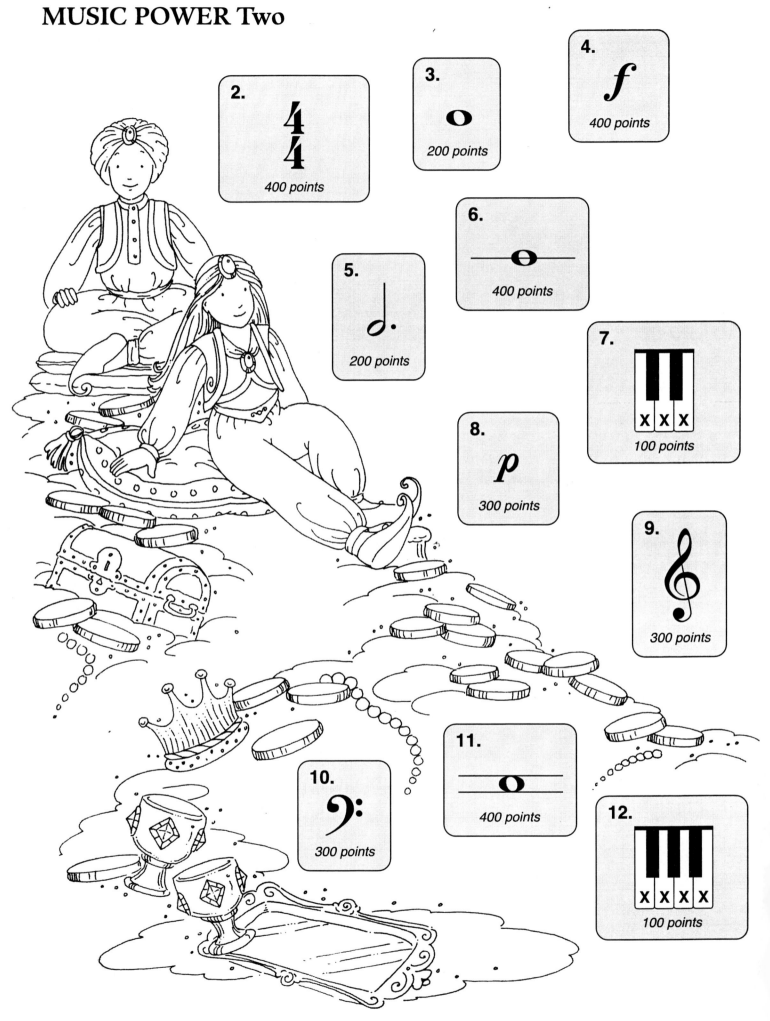

2. 400 points

3. 200 points

4. 400 points

5. 200 points

6. 400 points

7. 100 points

8. 300 points

9. 300 points

10. 300 points

11. 400 points

12. 100 points

Music Race—Game Board

Winner!

Place Token Here

Music Race—Question Cards

---

1. 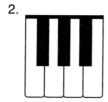 THIS IS A GROUP OF
____ BLACK KEYS.

Move 1 space.

2. THIS IS A GROUP OF
____ BLACK KEYS.

Move 1 space.

3. THIS IS A
_____
NOTE.

Move 3 spaces.

---

4. THIS IS A
_____
NOTE.

Move 3 spaces.

5. THE _____
_____ COMES
AT THE END
OF THE MUSIC.

Move 2 spaces.

6. THE _____
SIGN MEANS TO
PLAY THE MUSIC
AGAIN.

Move 2 spaces.

---

7. **A B C D E F G**

THESE ARE THE LETTERS OF THE
_____ ALPHABET.

Move 1 space.

8. NAME THE KEY.

Move 2 spaces.

9. NAME THE KEY.

Move 3 spaces.

---

10. NAME THE KEY.

Move 3 spaces.

11. NAME THE KEY.

Move 2 spaces.

12. NAME THE KEY.

Move 3 spaces.

---

13. NAME THE KEY.

Move 3 spaces.

14. NAME THE KEY.

Move 4 spaces.

15. *p*

THIS SYMBOL MEANS
TO PLAY
_____.

Move 4 spaces.

---

16. *f*

THIS SYMBOL MEANS
TO PLAY
_____.

Move 3 spaces.

17. THIS IS A
_____
NOTE.

Move 3 spaces.

18. $\frac{3}{4}$

THIS IS CALLED A
_____
_____.

Move 4 spaces.

---

19. THIS IS A
_____
NOTE.

Move 3 spaces.

20. THIS IS A
_____
CLEF SIGN.

Move 3 spaces.

21. THIS IS A
_____
CLEF SIGN.

Move 3 spaces.

---

22. *Move*
2
FREE SPACES

23. *Move*
3
FREE SPACES

24. *Move*
4
FREE SPACES
